A

Subtle

Sense

For Gran

Contents

Prologue 1

1. The Start 6
2. Dates 16
3. August 29
4. Granny Part I 35
5. Spirits 40
6. The Parallel World 56
7. Granny Part II 61
8. Dreams Part I 67
9. Seeking Guidance 78
10. Illness 85
11. A Troubled Spirit 94

12. Granny Part III	104
13. The Unexplained	120
14. Dreams Part II	127
15. 'And the rest will come'	140
Acknowledgements	145

Cover photo: *Gerry Hand*

Prologue

What can you call it, a Sixth Sense? Psychic ability? Or just coincidence?

I was never confident or comfortable using any of those words. I read about someone calling it the 'subtle sense' once and I thought, you know what, that sounds about right for me.

Already I can guess, scepticism has entered your mind. Proof is needed or it's all a load of baloney, right? That's a good sign. All the best analysts are sceptics. All the greatest leaders didn't think they could lead. If you don't question yourself then you will never learn. That's something I'm getting more used to now than ever before. I've also learned that not everyone is a believer; in God; in faith; in science; in physics; in themselves. But everyone comes from the same place, whether that be outer space, a Godly creation or mere dust - we are *all* connected through our energies.

Have you ever met someone for the first time and felt like you've known them all along? Or dreamed of a particular something and then, lo and behold, the next day it happens? Or even had a fleeting thought and it became a reality? Coincidence is only a word. These things most certainly do happen for a reason. It's figuring out that reason at that particular time or later on down the line that gives us a sense of fulfilment. That, ladies and gentlemen, is your subtle sense.

I was an awkward child growing up. My mother had a difficult time with me from the womb right up until the day I left home. I was a real tomboy with no fear. My older brother, who was my best friend throughout my childhood, never saw anything unusual in me. I was just one of the lads, hanging out with him and my cousins who were all boys too of similar age.

We had a wonderful childhood growing up in the countryside of County Monaghan, running through the fields, playing football and rounders and picking the plums with my father in late Autumn.

My mother feared I would be born with birth defects as a result of the Chernobyl disaster of the same year. It was the fear of many mothers that particular year. But it wasn't to be, thankfully. I was two weeks overdue and it took two days for me to make my entrance into this world. I had a squashed nose and a strawberry bump on the side of my head. My mother always said 'you fought your way into this world and you've been fighting your way through it ever since' a comment that only really resonated with me in my twenties.

I have never felt alone my entire life. Isn't that a mad thing to say?! My whole life I have always felt something special next to me that no one else could sense, a male energy watching over me and keeping me company. I never dared tell anyone because how could I explain something I could feel but not see? How did I know it was a male if I couldn't describe them? I just knew. I used to call him my guardian angel because we had learned about them in school but, deep down, I always knew he was more than that. This was a part of me that was between two worlds. My male energy growing up alongside me, guiding me on my journey with a protective shield all the way.

I never named him. It was my mother who did that many moons later.

The Start

I think it's important to note, from the start, that I think I'm still a big kid at heart today, only sometimes mind! My parents were convinced I had ADHD growing up. I could never sit still. I was always full of energy and doing things that got me into trouble. I was never afraid of breaking the rules or the consequences that came of it when I did so. I just wanted to have a good time and enjoy myself. Some people called it boldness – I liked to think of it as fun! One example my mother tells anyone who comes to visit: 'When Aideen was 11 years old, she got suspended for kissing the boys in the sandpit!' Only now she has added an extra part where apparently I charged them all two pence each. For the record, I didn't. I mean if I was going to charge, I would have charged a lot more than two pence!

My parents were teachers - my father a secondary school teacher who later became Principal and my mother a primary school teacher, later to become a Deputy Principal. We had a strict upbringing but had the happiest of childhoods. We had curfews, chores to do around the house, no sweets unless it was a special occasion, no discos until we were 15 years of age.

We were spoiled in other ways though. Mam and Dad took us on holidays to France every summer where we would spend long days playing in the pool, meeting new friends and dining out most evenings. We would go to mass every Sunday and then head out on little spins around the countryside after dinner. Like many Irish households at that time, we said our prayers after Glenroe on a Sunday night and always had our homework done for the following day.

I never really had a best friend at school or for that matter through most of my childhood. I was very much a loner and didn't mind it at all. I loved sports and music. All that energy was put to good use when I was playing Camogie or Gaelic football. And one particular year, during Primary School, Santa Claus brought me set of drums. Mam said he obviously wanted to help keep me out of the house! I was allowed to convert the loft in our garage into my own little space so that's where I hung out most of the time playing my music. I was a big Guns n' Roses fan. Nowadays it's more Adele and Celine Dion. Big difference!

I like to think I was an ordinary kid growing up. Yes, a bit naughty but I liked to tell people there would have been no entertainment in my house if I hadn't have done half the things I did! So, when my subtle sense began to take hold, it was understandable to think, from another person's point of view, that I was just making it all up out of badness. But it continued into my later years and there was no more room for excuse.

The subtle sense has come to me in many forms over the years since my childhood. I have had vivid dreams, strong sensations or 'feelings', flash visions, spirit visitations and dates.

Dates you ask? A number that would come to my mind and sometimes the name of a month. This began from about age thirteen upwards. Before that though, I can recall feeling spirits around me at different times. When we would go plum picking up the fields with Dad in late October each year, we would always go to a particular tree that hung over a derelict cottage in the middle of nowhere. The roof had caved in many years before and the stone walls were beginning to crumble and merge into part of the countryside. Every time we reached this house, I could always sense a young lady near me, a vision, always seeing her in my mind. She was wrapped in a black shawl with an off-white apron wrapped around her waist. She had beautiful long, wavy, red hair and freckles galore. She wore a light blue patterned dress underneath, mixed with pastel colours. I could never see her feet. I could feel she was a mother and yet I never sensed anyone but her there. I always saw the same pattern, year after year. She was there, with basket in hand, walking the mucky stone-ridden laneway from this cottage towards town. That was it. Never anything more than that vision and then she would be gone.

I never thought much of it and I certainly never told my Dad or my brother for fear of being ridiculed. It was only when I was about eleven years of age that I felt that same sense once again.

I always believed our home had a connection to the past as well, that our house had been built on something historical, particularly the west side of the house. I used to share a bedroom with my brother and then later on with my little sister, until I left for college. This bedroom was situated on the west side of the house above our little sitting room. From our room, you could hear cars coming and going, visitors knocking at the front door and anyone out in the garden. Over the years, at times, my sister and I could hear footsteps walking around the outside of the house in the dead of night. We always presumed it was our Dad out looking for something or some poor drunken neighbour at the wrong house. Whenever we asked the following morning we were told we were imagining it.

I started to suffer from bad headaches while sleeping in that room. My mother decided to get a dowser to look at it and he gave us a black box that would correct the energies in the house or something along those lines. It worked for a little while but then something happened, later on, that would change that room forever. I will tell you about that a little later in the book. I still believe that there is a history to be found in the earth around or under our home. Maybe someday, long after we're gone, someone will find out.

Growing up, I was very close to my cousin Eimear and she would often come to visit or stay over. She was like the big sister I never had, telling me all about make-up, clothes, boys and other 'cool' things that I would never have learned about otherwise! On one particular occasion, when I was about eleven, at a family gathering for my Grandfather's anniversary, we had the obligatory mass and then dinner afterwards in a local hotel. Eimear, my brother and I managed to sneak off after dessert. Eimear had robbed a cigarette from her Dad and wanted to smoke it somewhere away from the hotel so we walked out the road a little, to where the old Famine Workhouse stood. To an adult this was just a huge, dilapidated building falling into decay but, to a child, this was the dream adventure trail.

The other two decided that this was the place to hide from view to try out the cigarette. As they walked towards the main entrance of the building, my heart jumped in my chest and I felt unwell. I felt there was a bad feeling attached to the place but, to show face, I followed them into the building. There was coldness as soon as we entered and an eerie quiet that floated through each derelict room. Eimear proceeded toward a set of dodgy looking stairs that wound their way up to the second floor and into a very large open room. The rafters were hanging from the ceiling and the holes in the roof allowed the birds to use it as they pleased. As the other two reached the top of the stairs, I stopped halfway and could not go any further. There was a strong pressure pushing against me and I was too weak to carry on. I told the others to go on and I sat where I was. As I sat there, I felt that same sense of someone next to me. This time it was a little girl of similar age to myself. She looked awful: ragged clothes, worn face and cheekbones jutting out from her pale skin. She had straggly hair and big dark eyes. As sickly as she looked, her eyes gleamed with happiness and warmth. I didn't feel afraid, just sad. And, just as soon as she was there, she was gone. I called out to the two to hurry up and I ran from the building as fast as my little legs could take me. They came minutes later without a care in the world. I never told them what I had seen, not to this day, believe it or not.

Years later, when the Workhouse was given the restoration it deserved, I learned its real history. That large room we had made our way towards, all those years before, was originally the girls dormitory during famine times and many had passed away there due to hunger or disease. Some of the girls, who were part of the assisted emigration programme of the time, are now named on the newly painted walls of that dorm and the room has been blessed during a beautiful service to mark those who had perished. The building itself is magnificent and well worth a visit.

Dates

This is one I still can't get my head round at times. Random numbers just come to me from nowhere. It's hard to describe but, basically, when I was moving towards my thirteenth birthday, numbers played a large role in my subtle sense. It was sometimes very easy to understand and, at other times, I had to work out what it meant and for whom it was meant.

My mother was a teacher at the time, teaching first class. She taught in a well-known country school and loved her job very much. She treated the children as if they were her own and always put her whole heart into making their time at school fun and memorable. One day, after work, she collected all three of us (we had a little sister called Sarah now) from our respective schools. She never uttered a word the whole way home and I knew something bad must have happened at her own school that day. The normal routine was that we went straight to our homework as soon as we got home and today was no different. It was only when Dad arrived home from work and we sat down to have our dinner together that Mam got upset. She's a sensitive soul even to this day, wears her heart on her sleeve. When she was finally able to speak, she told us of how a little boy in her class was very sick and needed our prayers. She said he had leukaemia and that doctors were doing everything they could to make him better. I remember my father reassuring her that all would be ok. None of the children said anything. We just let her talk and we ate the remainder of our dinner in silence. But in my mind, already, a number had come to me and a month. It was a date in late June. When we were excused from the dinner table, I ran upstairs and circled the date on the calendar on my bedroom wall. My sister and I were sharing a room at the time and she saw what I had done and asked me why. I told her bluntly, with no real understanding at the time that 'something was going to happen that little boy on this date'. She never questioned it. She didn't even blink. It seemed as though she just understood.

I never thought about it again after that and as my first year in secondary school came to a close, I was shipped off to the Gaeltacht in Donegal for three weeks. The day of my departure was quite dramatic. My mother's Uncle Hughie had passed away the previous Friday and his funeral took place on the Sunday I was to leave. I remember racing from the Church to get some food and then straight to the bus outside my school. I remember having a good old cry on the bus on the way up as I felt sorry for my Granny watching her bury her brother. A girl from my class came and gave me a tissue and comforted me as we continued our journey northwards.

I didn't settle all of that first week in Donegal. Each morning we had to take a rickety old mini bus to and from our boarding house to the school. I recall on the first Friday I was there, sitting on my own on the bus on the way home from school. The sun was splitting the trees and there was great excitement on the bus as many had planned to go to the beach that evening. But not me, I remember being in a world of my own, oblivious to the background noise on the bus and staring blankly out the window. I felt a shiver tingle up my spine, that feeling some describe as someone 'walking over your grave' and my tummy was doing somersaults. I knew something was wrong and I sensed it was something to do with Granny back home. Now, there were no such things as mobile phones or emails back then. It was posted letters or, if you were really nice to Bean an Tí, she'd allow you to use her house phone for five minutes. When I got back to the house, I quietly went into Nuala (Bean an Tí) and asked her could I call home as I had a feeling something wasn't right. She agreed and handed me the cordless house phone. I went into one of the empty bedrooms and proceeded to dial my home number. No answer. Odd I thought, it was late on a Friday afternoon in June, someone was usually there. I then rang my Granny's number and it was my mother who answered. I could hear a lot of talking in the background and instantly knew there was a full house of people there, for some reason. My heart sank. 'Mammy?' I asked. 'Aideen', she replied. 'Why are you calling here?' When I told her about my 'feeling' and asked if everything was alright, she hesitated and eventually answered with a 'yes, of course.' She said that everyone had gathered to visit Granny to see how she was after the previous weekend. I had no reason to doubt her so I finished the conversation and handed the phone back to Bean an Tí. I didn't sleep that night. I remember lying in my bunk bed staring at the ceiling thinking something didn't add up. It left my mind the following day as we were céilí bound and the craic was mighty!

When parent's weekend arrived the following week, I was so excited to see my family. Other relatives arrived first on the Friday night. They were staying at the local hotel and called on me to come join them for dinner that night as Mam and Dad wouldn't be up until Sunday morning. Free meal I thought so I was there with bells on! We'd been living on salads in the boarding house up until then. When I reached the hotel that evening, I had brought a friend along with me for company as she was also looking forward to a slap up meal. My relations had left word at the reception desk that I was to go up to their room to see them first. It didn't faze me at the time and my friend was happy to stay in the lobby until I returned. When I got to the room, I was so happy to see them and there were hugs all round. Just as soon as I closed the door, they looked at me gravely and asked me to take a seat. My heart sank. Something bad was going to emerge and I didn't know what to expect. 'Aideen, we have some bad news for you.

Your Uncle Georgie (Gran's last living brother) died a few days ago.' I remember thinking they had the wrong name. Hadn't I been at Uncle Hughie's funeral before coming to Donegal! 'No, No, Georgie died a week after Hughie and your mother said we weren't to tell you until now.' I could feel the tears stinging my eyes but refusing to fall. I asked what had happened and they replied that they had found him on Friday morning of last week when he hadn't answered his door or phone calls. My cousin had to climb in through a bedroom window. He must have been lying there all night. Still the tears wouldn't fall. I immediately thought back to the rickety old bus. The journey back to the boarding house from school the previous Friday. I had been right. Something was wrong at home. They must have just found him when I got the 'feeling'.

After a few minutes, I left the room and quietly made my way back down to the lobby where, upon seeing my friend, the floodgates opened. I didn't know if I was crying for my deceased uncle, my granny's sadness or the fact that I hadn't been told until then. When my parents came to visit later, I remember my mother sitting next to me on a rock looking out at the beautiful coastline and asking me why I had called Granny's house that previous Friday? How did I know something was up? I couldn't give her an answer because I honestly didn't know myself.

I don't remember much of the last week in the Gaeltacht. I just wanted to go home at that stage and forget all about it. When the day did arrive for us to pack up and leave, I was the first one on the bus! My Dad was waiting in his car at the school gates when we returned, Sarah in the backseat with her little face pressed to the window waiting to see me. I was so happy to be home. I got into the car and asked where Mam was. Dad replied, "She's gone to the funeral of her little student that passed away." I was a little taken aback by the news but the long journey had tired me so Dad's words hung in the air. It was only when we got back to the house and Sarah followed me to our room that she quietly whispered "Aideen, look" and she pointed to the calendar on the wall. There, sure enough was the circled date I had pencilled in a while before. I looked back to Sarah with a quizzed look and she said "that's the day Mammy's little student passed away. You were right."

Coincidence. Right? Had to be. Well that's what I told myself anyway.

A year passed and nothing out of the ordinary had happened since that last unnerving episode. I was a spotty teenager growing into my skin and hanging out with new friends. I wore Doc Martens with double denim and thought I was the bees' knees. One evening, at home, I was playing games with Sarah in our room when the house phone rang. It was my mother's cousin calling to tell us that her mother (Mam's Aunt) was unwell, the only sibling Gran had left after the passing of her two brothers the summer before. I remember tiptoeing out of my room and sitting half way down the stairs to hear the conversation more clearly. Mam was taking in all the information and consoling her cousin on the other end of the line. "Cancer" "Not looking good." My mind was already in motion, a date in August came to me and I went back into my room and scribbled it on my calendar. I remember thinking – 'let's just wait and see now'. Sarah questioned me about the new date when she saw it later on that day. I told her I believed we would be at a funeral that day. Then I tried to push it to the back of my mind and get on with my day.

As the weeks passed and we came into the month of August, my Mam's sister Meg came to visit for a few days. Meg's a cool aunt. She's extremely intelligent and family means the world to her. While she was with us that time, Mam and Dad decided that they would look into taking a weekend break away together to celebrate their wedding anniversary. They looked into possible dates right up until the end of the month. When they decided they would go on the second last weekend of the month, I said aloud 'I wouldn't do that if I were you, you're going to be at a funeral that weekend.' They both looked at me, bewildered, and I knew that I'd opened a can of worms. Nonsense in their opinion I thought. I was attention seeking and looking to cause hassle. I tried my hardest to make them understand. I even took the calendar down from my wall and showed them. Told them whose funeral we would be attending. I went to the point of dragging poor little Sarah into it as back up but she wasn't to be believed either. They booked their weekend away, regardless. It was my aunt Meg who followed me from the room afterwards and said that she believed me. That meant the world to me, that someone other than my little sister, a grown up, didn't think I was going insane or acting the maggot.

When that particular weekend arrived, I was sitting at home watching TV on my own when the phone rang. It was a relative ringing to tell my Mam that their aunt had just passed away. As I was alone in the house, he left it to me to tell Mam when she got home. I asked what the funeral arrangements were and hung up shortly afterwards. No sooner had I put the phone down when it rang again, I picked up and it was my aunt Meg on the other end of the line in a raised, excited voice saying "You knew, you knew, oh my God! You have a gift Aideen, you have a gift." Needless to say, my parents cancelled their weekend away and we were standing at a graveside on the date that was written in black and white on my calendar. That incident was never mentioned in our house again.

I never really had numbers or dates come to me much after that. But, in saying that, more recently I have had the number 66 go through my mind a lot and it seems to pop into my life via signs, advertisements, written in places or even mentioned in conversation by others. I've tried researching various things to do with the number but nothing is making sense to me. 66 books in the bible? Verse 66? Or is it someone's age? Who knows! I'm sure it will show itself in good time. I'm in no rush to find out what it means anyway. It can be unnerving!

August

I used to dread the month of August when I was growing up. It seemed to go by so quickly and before I knew it, I was back at school. August in our house was similar each year. We'd make the most of the long evenings with a barbecue or playing with the other kids in the neighbourhood until darkness fell and our parents yelled at us to come home. Mam and Dad's wedding anniversary fell in this month as did my late Grandfather's Anniversary. I always dreaded the latter event, in particular, because it meant school was only around the corner. My mother came from a large family and this anniversary was a time for most of her siblings and their families to come together and catch up over dinner. We got to hang out with our cousins who we might not see for another year after that. I got to hang out with Eimear and I used to really look forward to that. This particular August, Eimear was to stay in our house after the dinner as her parents were away on holidays. I was so excited. She was going to be in Sarah's bed and we'd probably end up talking and giggling all night.

As we all sat down in the hotel to eat our dinner, Eimear was seated to my right and my father and brother were in front of us along with another cousin or two. After we finished our main course and the chat was in full flow, I found myself feeling a little queasy so I excused myself to go to the bathroom. As I walked the length of the hall towards the bathroom, I felt my stomach begin to turn and a sudden throbbing pain hammering through my head. I made it as far as the bathroom where I was doubled over in pain. I managed to run the cold tap and fill the sink with water. Don't ask me why but instinct told me to just dip my hands into the freezing water to calm and cool me down. It worked and still works today. When I began to feel like myself again, I started to question whether it was food poisoning or a bug of some sort. Then, like a bolt of lightning, Eimear came into my mind, something to do with Eimear. Something was wrong. Was there great pain or the like coming to Eimear? I needed to get back to the dining room and warn her. When I got back to my seat, Eimear took one look at me and said I looked awful and asked if I was alright. I told her something was wrong and she presumed I meant that I was ill but I repeated myself by saying that something was wrong and it was something to do with her. I could see she was worried now and told me to 'whisht' as her parents were away and she didn't want to be worrying about them. I said "No, it's not your parents, it's something else". At that very moment, Eimear's sister Aoife, who had been absent from the meal, came bursting through the double doors of the dining room. She looked troubled and my heart sank. I knew what was coming. Eimear ran towards her and all I remember was her crumbling to the floor sobbing heavily. Aoife had just informed her that her friends had been killed in a car accident. When I heard the news, I sank into my chair and the room, the noise, the people all became a blur. Shock. My mother helped to lead Eimear to a chair and gave her a drink of sorts. When I finally found my feet, I sheepishly stepped towards her. She never took her eyes off me as I walked and when I knelt by her feet, she just muttered the words "how did you know?"

I shrugged my shoulders. I felt guilty. I felt like I had some part to play in this awful tragedy even though I knew, of course, that I didn't. I just couldn't understand what was happening and why it was happening to me. What was going on with my mind, my body. Why was I the weirdo? Eimear cried the whole night through. I let her talk and talk for hours and in the early morning Mam gave her some rescue remedy to help calm her nerves. I will never forget that night as long as I live. I felt that I had this secret and the people that I loved the most would now look at me differently as my secret was starting to show itself.

Granny

Part One

I was very close to my Grandmother on my Mam's side. We had always got on well and she was like a second mother to us, the sixth member of our family really. She was a lovable character. Small with perfectly permed golden hair that she allowed turn grey in her later years. Her eyes were grey and held a glow that would light up a room when she walked in. She had a big heart and, by golly, she loved to talk! She would tell us stories for hours upon end of the 'good 'aul days'. She was extremely religious too and never missed a day of prayer. Many of my subtle sense stories involve her so you will be hearing her name a lot in this book.

I recall one evening at home rushing to finish my homework as Father Ted was going to be on the TV and it couldn't be missed! As I packed my books and copies away into my bag, I suddenly had a vision of my Granny saying the number 97 to me. It came out of nowhere. I thought nothing of it but the more the evening carried on, it continuously popped into my mind. It was like a voice in my head telling me this number was important. I wrote it down in the back of my journal before going to sleep that night and I wrote Granny with a question mark next to it. I told Sarah too as 'back up' but she couldn't make head nor tail of it either. I did ask my Granny about it in due course but she had no idea what I was on about. She told me to have a 'titter-a-wit,' whatever that meant!

In July 2001, we went on a family holiday to France. Just the four of us. My brother had a summer job at the time and wanted to stay at home. We had rented out a mobile home and the weather promised to be fabulous. We even made new friends that were also from our hometown and it was a holiday like no other. Every evening Sarah and I would play games with our parents or go and see what the entertainment was like in the resort. One evening when there was a shower of rain, Dad took out a deck of cards and we proceeded to play 'Switch' in the lounge area of the mobile. My mother was preparing dinner in the kitchen next to us. I had my back to her and was facing my father. As the game progressed, I started to feel the tingle up my spine, the shiver through my bones and the sudden alarming emotion that shot through my body. Dad could see my mood change and shot me a glance. I didn't speak for a few seconds and when I eventually did, all that came out was "Something's wrong with Granny. We need to call home." I could feel my mother's eyes bore into my back. Dad sighed but knew what had to be done. The dinner was left in the sink and we were marched to the nearest payphone (still no mobiles back then!) As Sarah and I stood outside, peering in at my parents fiddling with the dial on the phone, I kept thinking 'please God, don't let this be it. Not now.' We heard my brother pick up the phone in Granny's house and Mam wasted no time in getting to the point. My brother told Mam that Gran had had a nasty fall earlier that day and broken her shoulder but that she was absolutely fine and we were not to be worrying. Mam's sister had arrived to take care of her so we could rest assured she wasn't going to 'pop her clogs' anytime soon. I'll never forget my mother staring back at me in frustration through the glass of that phone box. It was unnerving. I decided there and then that I would start to keep things like that to myself from then on and maybe this thing, whatever it was that I had, could just be ignored.

Spirits

For anonymity purposes, I refer to someone in this chapter as 'T'.

The years passed and I was preparing to go to college. I had received my exam results on a wet Wednesday morning in August 2004 and knew Dublin was the destination for my future studies but there was partying and celebrations to be had before that! I had learned to ignore my subtle sense at this stage. If I felt a tingling in my spine, I wouldn't allow it to take hold. I would shake it off and turn on some music. If I had a vision, I wouldn't act on it or tell anybody. I wouldn't allow it to stay in my mind afterwards nor would I go looking for answers. I always kept busy and by now I had a weekend part time job as housekeeper for the local priests, yes, like a real life 'Mrs Doyle' from the TV programme 'Father Ted'!

Two days after our exam results were out, I was told by my mother to go to Dublin to look for accommodation before starting my degree at St. Patrick's College. My friend Lorraine and I decided to make a day of it and we saw as many houses as we could with the time we had. When we stopped for a bite to eat in Graingers pub off Griffith

Avenue, I was devouring a dirty fry up when my mobile phone began to ring (Nokia 3310 - it was the biz!) It was my mother. I looked at Lorraine and laughed. I said – 'if she hears us in a pub now, she's going to think we're not doing any house hunting at all!' I answered anyway and waited for the string of questions to follow. But there was none. My mother sounded very serious. "Aideen, where are you?" I proceeded to tell her and asked if everything was ok. She hesitated and then replied with "Your friend 'T' was killed in a car accident this morning."

Boom. Just like that. My world came crashing down. Poor Lorraine couldn't fathom why my face had suddenly turned white and my hands were shaking. Even the barman had stopped to look over. I don't remember much after that only he came over with a stiff drink and I think my brother came on the phone to console me. My only thought was to get home as soon as possible. The earliest bus wasn't for another three hours. I walked like a zombie around the streets of Dublin counting down the clock, calling the group of friends that would be going through the same emotions as myself. Nothing worked. I was at a loss.

Lorraine was like an angel that day. I don't know how she kept it together but she looked after me every step of the way until we got back on home ground. My mother picked me up from the station and drove me home. The house was empty when we got back and Mam told me to go up and have a shower, that I needed to wash today off and that she'd make me something to eat before I went to be with my friends. I stood in that shower motionless and just kept going over and over the news in my mind. I had no sense of it coming. Or did I and I chose to ignore it? I had pushed the feelings and senses away for long enough that now I felt I was being punished and that maybe, just maybe, I could have seen this coming had I accepted things as they were. I was shell shocked to the core of my very being. Not only was I grieving for my friend, I was selfishly grieving for myself.

The memorial service and funeral were like an out of body experience to me. I was not fully there at all. I can't even tell you what I was wearing or what was said or sung in church that day. I took time off from my housekeeping job and began moving my stuff to Dublin. I felt that by leaving to start anew elsewhere, it would make everything easier. It worked, but only for a little while.

Exactly two weeks after T's death I was at home asleep in my bed dreaming of burning the dinner for the priests the following day as I was returning to work for the first time since it had happened. I remember clearly waking myself up and thinking thank God that was only a dream. I could see Sarah was still asleep in her bed so I decided not to turn on the light and to go back to sleep. I turned over in the bed and just as I did, there she stood in my view. Dressed in a navy hoodie, beige tracksuit bottoms and her hair tied back in a ponytail. Her eyes were glistening and she had her Winnie the Pooh mobile phone up to her left ear. She looked so content. Her mouth broadened into a big smile and with that, she began to disappear. I could feel myself begin to sob. I put my hand out to touch her as she went but there was nothing. I could hear Sarah moving in her bed across the way. She mumbled something and I said "T is here." Without a second thought, she was up and out of her bed over to me. I was shaking uncontrollably and she ran to get Mam and Dad. I was brought into the bathroom and laid on the floor where Mam kept wetting my lips with sugared water. Sarah explained to them what happened but they couldn't take it in. They kept saying 'it's only the grief. She's in delayed shock.' My brother must have heard the commotion as he came out of his room to see what was going on. When Sarah told him what had happened, they both went into the room to check for anything. When they returned to the bathroom, they told my parents that the room was icy cold. You could see your own breath in front of you. I didn't sleep in that room for quite a while after that.

My parents refused to believe that we had had a visitation in our house. We argued over it quite a bit in the weeks that followed and I grew very bitter towards their disbelief. I recall writing a letter to my mother about it because I thought somehow that might get through. What she did after that letter changed me for the better.

It was a Sunday evening and I was back in the bedroom with my sister listening to music. The room was still icy cold and no amount of heaters or radiators were doing any good. There was a knock at the front door and my mother's sister Bernie (Eimear's Mum) had come to visit. Bernie is great. She loves her reiki and spiritual retreats. She has an open mind on everything and believes that we should all live our lives to the full. She puts it in a much more profound way but you get the picture. She had come to speak to me at my mother's request. I guess the letter had worked in a way I hadn't imagined.

Bernie came up to our room and sat with Sarah and myself on my bed, near where T had appeared. She took out a deck of cards and explained that they were angel cards. I had never heard of such a thing but I was intrigued. The first thing she said, before explaining to me how the cards worked, was 'I was told what happened here and I believe you. We're going to figure out why she came to you.' With that, she laid the full deck of cards out in front of me, face down and told me to ask the question in my mind and to pick a card when I was ready but only when I felt guidance towards a particular card. I closed my eyes for what felt like an eternity and simply asked 'Why?' I then hovered my hand over the deck with my eyes still closed and waited. I waited and waited. The other two never made a sound. I think they were waiting with as much anticipation as myself. Eventually I felt a warm pressure pushing my hand down and when I opened my eyes, I had pushed a card away from the others. Bernie jumped straight in and took it from me, careful not to reveal its contents. She asked me what question had I asked and I told her I wanted to know why T came back, why she had come to me. Sarah was sitting behind Bernie peering over her shoulder as she looked at the card in front of her. Both their eyes widened and mouths dropped. "What?" I shouted. No reply. "WHAT??" They started smiling and looked at me. Bernie whispered "You've got a gift kid" and handed me the card. It was the Angel of Communication with a little illustration of two angels speaking to each other by telephone, one in heaven and the other down on earth. This time it was my eyes that widened and my smile that beamed across at them. It was a wonderful feeling and I immediately felt this loving warmth wrap around me. T was ok. She was telling me that she was ok and that I had something I needed to use. No more ignoring it.

I still have those angel cards. They have never let me down when I needed them and I've shared them with others when they needed them too.

From that day on, I decided to reopen myself to my subtle sense. I knew it was going to take time but I was prepared to try my best and see what would come of it. I don't think there is any real way of teaching oneself to be open to things. It's just a gradual thing that takes practise. For me, I began to pray again. I prayed to T a lot. I tried not to judge or be harsh which is very difficult at times as most people know. I spoke to whoever might be listening on the other side and asked for guidance and grace. I allowed the old sensations to take hold but I couldn't place who or what they were about so I knew I still had a long way to go. I think at this point, my parents were starting to come around to the fact that I had something and I needed to let it do its thing.

In April 2006, in my second year of College, I was sharing an apartment with my old pal Lorraine. It was on the second floor of an old terraced house about five minutes from the college. The apartment was so cosy and we had many good memories there. We were sharing a huge bedroom which had an old fireplace in the corner. Lorraine had a habit of sleep talking (she'll kill me for saying that!). I have always been a light sleeper but I was well used to her nocturnal habits and we were nearing the end of the academic year.

This particular night, she sat upright in her bed and pointed straight at the bedroom door shouting 'Aideen look, look!' I sat up in my bed and looked over but couldn't see anything. We always left the door open. It led into a little hallway between our front door and the kitchen. As we were on the second floor, there was a main front door on ground level. I whispered back to her "Lorraine, there's nothing there, you're sleep talking. Go back to sleep." She shouted back, "I'm not, I'm wide awake and there is a man standing right there in our doorway." I was losing patience by now and jumped out of the bed, turned on the light and walked through the doorway twice to prove to her that there was nothing there. She looked at me and said "he was definitely there." I sighed loudly, switched off the light and went back into my bed. She turned on her side and not another word was spoken.

The following morning, Lorraine was reluctant to talk to me over breakfast so I tried to crack a joke about what had happened the previous night but she looked at me sternly and repeated what she had seen the previous night. 'I know what I saw Aideen. I wasn't asleep.' With that, she finished up and left for college. She intentionally didn't come back to the apartment for a week or so after that. I told my friends at college what had happened and they were as sceptical as me because they knew from my other tales that Lorraine had a habit of sleep talking.

However, a number of days later when I was asleep in the apartment by myself, I woke up to a noise outside my window. When I turned over in the bed to see what it was, there was a gentleman standing at the foot of my bed. He was dressed in unusual attire, almost servant like. He had a long white shirt on that wasn't tucked into his black trousers. Over the shirt was an open maroon coloured waistcoat. He had huge brown eyes with a buzzcut hairstyle and looked to be in his twenties or thirties. No word of a lie, I nearly wet the bed in pure fear. I was frozen and couldn't seem to move. When my eyes looked him up and down, top to bottom, I realised there was nothing below his shins. He was just floating in mid-air. I closed my eyes so tightly and started to pray. I did not want this person in my room or near me. I was so scared. After a few seconds, I opened my eyes and he was gone. Needless to say I did not sleep for the rest of the night. I turned on every light available and lay awake, counting down the minutes.

The following day I called Lorraine and before she had a chance to speak I asked her to describe the man she had seen the previous week. She described exactly the same person I had seen the night before. The hair stood on the back of my neck. I apologised profusely to Lorraine for not believing her and told her I would get in touch with our landlord as soon as possible. When I got off the phone to her, I called a friend from college, told her what had happened and she advised me to skip lectures and go straight to the college priest for help.

I did exactly that. The college priest was a guy called Fr. Eamon and he was a true gentleman. He blessed the apartment that evening and told me to research the history of the building with my landlord. We spoke for a while afterwards and he told me that we weren't the first to experience such events and we certainly wouldn't be the last. My landlord didn't have any history on the building other than he had purchased it from another man years before. He also said that nothing had ever happened like this before and was quite spooked himself. I never did find out who our visitor was or what it was he wanted but I like to think Fr. Eamon released him from whatever may have been holding him to the building.

Another encounter I had with the spirit world involved my sister and my mother this time. I was teaching in a school in Goatstown., Dublin at this time and was living in a nearby house with two boys. I had the box room and loved my little space. The home was a happy one and we all got on very well. One night when I was lying in my bed, a faceless lady spirit appeared standing next to the dresser at my bed. When I say faceless, I literally mean there was no face, just blackness around her head, like you would see when a TV crew blur out somebody's face on camera. She was dressed in black and was so thin that I thought this definitely wasn't human. She was extremely tall as well and never moved an inch. Within seconds, she vanished and I calmly got out of my bed and went downstairs. I told the boys and they of course thought I had lost my mind but went up to check the room regardless. There was nothing there and I took it on the chin that they thought I was dreaming.

When I went home that weekend, I wasn't going to mention it to my family as I really didn't know what it was or what it meant. It had scared me and I didn't want to do the same to them. However, my sister and I were chatting and she asked me if I had had any weird sensations or anything during the week. I said yes I had and enquired why she was asking. She said she had moved into my brother's old bedroom recently as it was warmer and when she had been studying in it one night – she saw a faceless woman standing in the corner. Well needless to say, I could feel the hair stand on the back of my neck! She described exactly the same thing I had seen and on the same night. We were quite freaked out about it all and we decided to tell our Mother what had happened. When we had rehashed the entire story to Mam, she didn't flinch or tell us we were imagining things. In fact, it was quite the opposite reaction to what we had expected. Mam whispered – 'I know, I think that same spirit was in my room too.' Now you can imagine after all my years of self-doubt and scepticism, to hear those words from my mother's mouth....well, it was a pivotal moment. We had no idea who this lady spirit was or what her intentions were, but from that day on, we never doubted one another again.

The Parallel World

Many people call it *Heaven*, the *Afterlife* up in the sky or the *Great Beyond*. I call it the Parallel World or the Next Dimension because that's exactly what it is. We don't go floating up to the clouds or anything like that. We simply cross over to another dimension, a parallel world. Like stepping through a mirror onto a completely different side and still being you but choosing to look like whatever age you were happiest. But it's also the *You* that other people remember. For example, you may be a young child to some or the face on an elderly woman to others depending on your life story and your relationship with them. I was told by a spirit once that the next life is all your happiest memories brought back together. That you feel nothing but peace and fulfilment, a floating sensation. She even let me feel it for a few seconds and all I can say is we shouldn't fear death. It's inevitable and what's waiting for us on the other side is like nothing you could ever imagine. Pure ecstasy. The tough part is right now, living.

I believe energies are what allow us to feel our loved ones and angels around us. I have learned that a woman's monthly cycle can have a huge influence on energies too. It is always around my time of the month that I found myself most in tune with my dreams and energies, like a heightened sense but with a calmer approach. I might not be describing it correctly but women are like a full moon, our moods can be altered by things beyond our control and for me, my monthly cycle allows me to be better in sync with myself, to trust whatever is happening or may happen. It's like a greater ability to connect.

Spirits of loved ones that have recently passed usually 'hang around' for a little while afterwards. They have crossed over but still feel a need to keep watch over those left behind. It's a natural thing I suppose. You can check out but you don't leave straight away. Those loved ones come in and out of both worlds when necessary. If you need them, they will be there. All you have to do is ask. My Granny told me once that prayer is mighty. She was right. Prayer is simply talking, having a conversation of sorts. So, if you think that you are talking to yourself at times, you're not! There is always someone listening.

I'm not a very religious person but I am spiritual. I don't believe in the different religions but I do respect those who have religious beliefs. We all need something to believe in, even atheists. They don't believe in God or other Gods but they still believe in something whether it is science, love, or just living a simple life. They are still believers like the rest of us. We are *all* connected.

Best advice I was given was 'not to try to understand this life but better to enjoy the journey into the next one.'

Granny

Part Two

From 2008 onwards, I was teaching full time in a primary school in Dublin. On the rare weekend, I would make it my business to go home and visit my family and friends but as most teachers know – sometimes you just don't have the energy to move after a week in the classroom. Weekends are about re-energising the batteries!

In mid-September 2012, I recall coming back to my apartment from work and having a heavy feeling that something was wrong at home. You know that feeling like someone has walked over your grave? I kept seeing Granny in my mind and I decided to call home and subtly ask if all was ok. My Mam answered the phone and after a little catch up, I asked about Granny. She said that she had the touch of a cold but was fine otherwise. I still wasn't happy when I put the phone down and decided I would text my sister to ask her to check in on Granny that evening. She was on her way home from stage school and would try to get into see her that night, with Mam, if she had a chance. I still wasn't satisfied! I decided to call the woman herself.

I dialled Gran's number and when she picked up, my heart sank. She sounded awful and wasn't making much sense. I tried to ask her if everything was ok but before she could answer, I heard her drop the phone to the ground and then nothing. Silence.

I whispered 'Granny'. Still nothing. Then I raised my voice and yelled her name. Still silence. Thank God for smart phones! With some quick thinking I put my call to her on hold and rang my Mam again on a new call. I explained to her what had happened and just as I was talking to her, I could hear Sarah coming through the front door in the background. Mam handed the phone to Sarah and ran to her car. I told her what had happened and she said she would go with Mam and call me back when they arrived at the house. I hung up and went back to the other call where there was still only silence.

It seemed like forever waiting for the two to arrive at the house and all I could do was speak down the line and hope that Gran could hear me. I told her everything was going to be ok and Mam was on her way, to hang in there. I asked

God not to take her like this. The best sound I have ever heard in my life was the sound of feet running towards her phone. Sarah picked up and said they were there. What followed was something I will never forget as long as I live.

I could hear my mother trying to wake her own mother up. Sarah described what was happening down the phone and told me they had already called Mam's brother and sister to come down and help. Granny wasn't stirring. I could hear heavy sobbing at this point and Sarah said it was Mam who was shaking Granny ferociously and crying her heart out. There was still no movement. I told Sarah to take over and keep the phone up to her ear. She went as far as giving Gran a little slap across the face and there was a little murmur. Thank God! I told Sarah to go down to the kitchen and get some sugared water to wet Gran's lips. She did that and Gran became a little more alert whilst Mam kept talking to her. By this time, others had arrived and took over nursing Granny.

Meanwhile, Sarah went back down to the kitchen, while still on the phone to me, and found the cause of the upset.

Gran had a routine of taking two painkillers every night for her arthritis. But since she had the flu at this time, she was taking more medication and it looked as if she had accidently taken too much. This was what had caused her to knock herself out, so to speak! She wasn't really herself after that fright and we later learned that this was the beginning of her journey into the next life.

Dreams

Part One

I never felt comfortable when spirits came to me. It scared me a lot and I didn't know how to handle it. I wanted to use my subtle sense but I felt I could never do that when visitations occurred. I needed to feel safe and happy to fully connect and that was when my dreams started to become part of the equation. They became my safe place. Occasionally, they also became little psychic predictions.

I remember the first time one of my dreams became a reality. I think it was August 2000. I had a very detailed dream about a submarine full of men sinking to the bottom of the ocean. These men were doing everything they could to fix the problem with the machine but it continued to sink. When I woke up the next morning, I came down to the kitchen for breakfast and happened to mention to my parents what I had dreamt about the night before. I remember my Dad looking at me very oddly. I asked him why he was looking at me like that and he said 'you were listening to the radio upstairs weren't you?' I replied that I hadn't. I'd literally gotten out of bed, put on my uniform and come straight down for breakfast. This was before the day and age of social media, when the only source of news in the morning was radio or TV. He had a questionable look in his eyes as if I were seeking attention. When I asked again what was wrong, my mother turned up the volume on the radio. The RTÉ news reader was speaking about a Russian submarine that had sank to the bottom of the ocean during a naval experiment. He went on to read that men were trapped alive inside and rescue teams were trying to get to them. I could feel my mouth fall open in shock. What were the chances of that after my dream! Then I understood why Dad had looked at me the way he did. He thought I'd made it all up for attention. I knew not to probe it further after that so I never mentioned it again. I followed the news on that story for days after. I hoped that they would find the men and save them but unfortunately they were never rescued, as it took quite a while for the submarine to be found or any investigation to be carried out afterwards. It was a few years later that I remember dreams becoming a more prominent factor with my subtle sense.

From about 2010 onwards, I looked to move away from teaching and started to focus on a lifelong ambition to work in radio. I spent my free time in the evening volunteering at a community radio station in Dublin. I loved it. It was an Irish language radio station and, as a fluent speaker, I was able to dust of the rustiness and enjoy conversing with others *as Gaeilge*. The sound technician for the station was a lovely guy and I remember coming in one evening and randomly saying to him – "I dreamt your wife was pregnant and it was a girl." He laughed and said absolutely not. I'd say he thought I was a right weirdo but a little while after that, he came back to me and told me his wife was indeed pregnant at the time I told him but they had no idea. And yes it turned out to be a girl. Coincidence?

Another incident occurred one Saturday morning. I woke up and remembered having had a vivid dream that I needed to do the lotto and the numbers 9 and 12 kept running through my mind. Now, I had never done the lotto in my life and wouldn't even know how to fill in the sheet. I went to my friend who did the lotto regularly. He explained that I could actually go to a betting shop and pick those two numbers to come out instead of an entire line of numbers and could win a couple of quid. So I said why not and my Dad wanted 'in' on the tip so we put down something like two euro each on both numbers to come out. We ended up winning nearly eighty euro between us. Dad thought this was the 'bees knees' and could I do it every week! Afraid not – it was a one off dream and I am no Mystic Meg, able to predict anything.

There was a night in late 2013 when I felt a spirit present in my room at home. I could feel it was a member of my extended family who had passed away years before. I knew that if I turned over in the bed I would see him so I just lay where I was, frozen. I didn't want to go through this again so I told him to come to me in my dreams. I would feel safer that way. He didn't.

The following morning the house phone rang with news about Mam's sister Marian. She had been sick a number of years before but had a relapse due to a fall the day before and was in a serious condition in hospital. It was her late husband I had sensed in my room the night before. We rushed to be by Marian's side and it was touch and go for a little while. When we were all gathered, chatting outside ICU, my aunt asked me what I thought was going to happen. I remember saying to her and others who were listening that it wasn't Marian's time to go yet. This was going to be a long journey for her. A journey that she is still on to this very day.

She was moved to a more comfortable facility when they stabilised her and is now under twenty-four hour care. I believe she is in something I call the twilight zone between this world and the next but not having a firm grasp on either. She, like Granny, has been involved in some of my strongest moments with my subtle sense. In one scenario, they both showed me together what exactly it is I have. I'll tell you about that a little later.

As I mentioned before, dreams became my new way of sensing things or situations. One such incident took place in January 2014. I had a very vivid dream about a friend of the family called Eileen who had passed away months before. She had been living abroad with her husband for many years and passed away suddenly due to a short illness. We had visited them once a year and I always had a soft spot for them so when she came to me in a dream, I was very aware that she needed to get a message to her husband. She was sitting in a bedroom that I had never seen before and spoke about things that made no sense to me. When I awoke from the dream I wrote everything down. I then went back to sleep and she came back to me again with more to say. When I got up the next morning, I re-read everything I had written down and decided that I would talk to my Mam about it. She encouraged me to tell Eileen's husband as it would probably make more sense to him. This was January and I knew we wouldn't be seeing him until March/April time so I agreed I would tell him face to face at that point. I was a little worried that he might be upset by it or that he'd think I was crazy but the messages seemed important so I promised Eileen I would do it.

Later that evening, when we had just finished our dinner, the house phone rang. I picked up and to my disbelief, it was Eileen's husband Ray! He never rang our house phone but today for whatever reason, he had. We spoke for a little while and I decided to bite the bullet and do a little digging into whether he believed in signs from the parallel world. The line went silent for a few seconds that seemed like minutes and eventually he answered with a low affirmative. He spoke of how he was finding white feathers in places you would never expect and that certain other things were happening in the apartment as if she were reminding him that she was still there. He said he always asked her to find him a parking space when he's out driving and she never failed! I breathed a sigh of relief and when he asked why I had asked the question, I told him that she had come to me the night before and that I had a message for him that I would relate to him face to face. Looking back now, it was probably the longest two or three months for him waiting on my arrival.

When we did meet, I showed him what I'd written down and described to him how she had come to me and the setting in which we were when she spoke to me. It all made perfect sense to him and what she had said was something only he knew of. I won't go into detail about it as it was private to them. I was really just happy to help if I could. He was a different man after that. It was like a weight had been lifted off his shoulders and he was able to continue on with his life knowing she was ok and he would be ok also.

I had another encounter with Eileen about a year after that. It was a variation on my subtle sense that overwhelmed me entirely. We were sitting in Ray's apartment on our annual visit and were having a few drinks. His mobile rang and he took the call while we sat around chatting. As he was talking, I suddenly felt very faint, as if I were about to slip into a deep sleep. The entire room went a very bright yellow and I could feel a ferocious heat coming from the empty couch to my left. In my mind, I could see Eileen sitting there, in all her glory, giving out that she hadn't been given a drink. I began sobbing uncontrollably and my mother who was sitting next to me grabbed my arm. Ray got off the phone and was of course concerned and asked what was wrong. I told them what was happening and what Eileen was saying. All the while this heat was still coming from the empty couch and hitting me like a blast of air.

Mam could feel it too. I felt like I had been hit with a steam roller and my legs were like jelly. It only lasted a minute, if even that, and then she was gone. She had just dropped in to say Hi. I had never experienced anything like it before. I couldn't even put a name on what had just happened but it had happened nonetheless. My sense was taking on a whole direction.

Seeking Guidance

I realised I was way out of my depth with all the 'goings on' and it was time to seek help from other like-minded people who could help me. I searched the internet, asked friends, read many books by various people who had experienced similar things to myself. I was given the name and number of a lady who could talk to me so I booked an appointment and took my friend Cathal with me for moral support. He never doubted me for a minute and wanted to help me in any way he could. Before attending the meeting we met with the lady's PA upon arrival. She was a lovely lady who I will call 'C'.

C explained to us that there were other appointments that had gone over their time and asked did we mind waiting. We were happy to sit and chat while we waited. As the minutes passed by, C came back over to apologise again for the delay and asked where we had travelled from. As she was talking, I could hear a man who seemed drunk shouting at the top of his voice from the back of the room. I looked at Cathal and C but they carried on talking regardless. I couldn't hear anything that was being said because he kept shouting, manically "It's Danny, tell her it's Danny!"

I thought no more about it and when C left us to take a phone call, I turned to Cathal and said "did you hear that man shouting at the top of his lungs?" Cathal looked at me puzzled and replied "What man?" I described what I'd heard and Cathal explained we were the only people left in the room. I insisted that I'd heard a man yelling, so when C came back over to us to say it was our turn to go in for our appointment, I asked her had she heard it. She hadn't and as she was speaking to me, the shouting started again. They still couldn't hear it. I can't explain why but, instinctively, I looked at C and asked her had she lost anyone in her life recently, a man by the name of Danny? Her face turned ashen. She whispered so lowly that I had to lean in close to hear her. "Yes, my father," she replied. I could see him now in my mind. A well-built man with thick hair standing behind her with his arms open as if expecting a hug and a bright light shining behind him. He looked to be protecting her from something. With her eyes as wide as could be, she looked at me, asking more information. I described what I was seeing and asked her why he was trying to protect her. Was there something wrong? C replied, "my daughter has just been diagnosed with an illness". C explained what exactly it was and I told her we were definitely meant to meet each other, that it may not be as bad as she thought. I told her I knew a friend of a friend who had gone through something similar and was cured. I gave her the phone number to speak with said friend and get the consultant's details. That was it. Throughout all of this, Cathal was just staring at me with his mouth wide open. I could only laugh!

I eventually got to meet the lady I had gone there to visit in the first place. She and I sat talking for quite a while and she told me that I had to believe in myself more, instead of looking for explanations to all the experiences, that it came from my Mum's side of the family and to embrace it openly without trying to force it. She asked if I ever felt a presence near me and I told her that I had always felt I was being watched over by a male spirit of sorts. She confirmed this and asked had I any large birthmarks on my body. I said I had. I had quite an unsightly looking thing on my right arm. She told me that this spirit was my twin brother and that this was the mark he had left on me and he had been with me ever since. I found that very hard to believe. So much so that I came home straight after that chat and spoke to my mother about it.

There was a history of twins on my mother's side of the family and they believed it had just skipped a generation. But she then recalled having to return to the hospital on the day of my christening as she felt like she was giving birth all over again. She had haemorrhaged and needed medical attention. She now believes that this lady was right and that I may indeed have had a twin. For me it would make sense as to why I've never felt alone or even why I always felt a male spirit watching over me. Who knows? But either way, my mother decided to name him Jamie. So I hope that in the parallel world, there might be another part of me there already.

I continued and still continue to seek guidance from anyone and everyone that can teach me or show me how to embrace this sense. Every person I have met has had their own story to tell and some were even able to heal people.

Some were able to see spirits all the time and converse with them openly. I felt like my sense was so mixed up, that I didn't have the qualities needed to understand what it was I was supposed to do with it. Maybe I was just supposed to let it do its thing and embrace it when it did. So that is exactly what I did.

Illness

When I was in my fourth year of teaching, I became very ill around Christmas time with an unknown virus that I couldn't shake off for two months. I was confined to my bed for the entire time and couldn't eat anything. All I could do was sip water, tea and 7 Up and even that was hard at times. I felt like my body was shutting down. My throat was closing up and I couldn't talk for more than a few seconds without coughing or getting sick. I couldn't sleep unless I was sitting upright. It was a very scary time and the doctors tried all types of medicines to help but in the end, bed rest was the only cure to flush it out of my system.

I was feeling a little better by late February and I went back to work. I was only back two weeks when I was in hospital for tests. I had found a lump in my right breast. When I went to my family GP, a hospital appointment was booked straight away. I remember feeling a sense of warmth and calmness come over me. I knew I was going to be fine but that I had to go through some obstacles before that could happen.

I was twenty-four years old when I walked into the Breast Cancer Clinic in St Vincent's Hospital, Dublin. I remember looking around the room and selfishly thinking to myself, I shouldn't be here. I'm probably the youngest person in the room. I was given a gown to put on and nervously; I put it on back to front! The nurse came in and smiled. She didn't tell me to fix it, she just let me walk on through to the examination room and told me to sit up on the bed. A doctor then came in and proceeded to inspect the body area where the lump was. After what seemed like an eternity, she told me she wanted to perform a biopsy. The calmness still remained, like a shield over my body. I agreed and signed the forms necessary.

The nurse was still in the room with us and began to ask me about my work. She was distracting me from the giant needle that was coming my way! It was very uncomfortable, painless but uncomfortable. When the doctor had finished, she said she couldn't give an immediate diagnosis and that my results would be back within two weeks and to let my life go on as normal, that they would be in touch as soon as possible. It was all a bit surreal to be honest. I went back, put my clothes on and walked out of the hospital to my car. I went to Mc Donalds in Stillorgan and ate a Big Mac to make myself feel better! It worked for all of ten minutes. Even with a sense of calmness, fear can creep in. Anyone who has had an unknown illness will know that a thousand different questions and worries go through your mind. What if it's this? How will I cope? That night I prayed so hard when I went to bed. I prayed that my subtle sense was right and that I was going to be fine.

When I went to work the following week, I confided in my teaching partner at the time. She had been an angel throughout my entire illness during the previous few months and now this was happening. She had her own worries to deal with at that time too but she always made time for others. She still does. She is one in a million.

I got a phone call from the hospital a few days after my tests. I was at work and asked my teaching partner to watch the class while I took the call. The doctor wanted to see me the following day. My heart sank. They wouldn't be ringing this soon if it was good news, I thought. They wouldn't tell me over the phone either so I agreed to attend the following day. My colleague tried to comfort me, saying all would be well and she would say a prayer for me.

It was a cold Friday morning. I remember my entire family sitting around the kitchen table in my house, as if they were at a funeral. I was the cheerful one trying to keep the mood light and cracking jokes. Mam asked if I had said my prayers and that whatever happened, they would be with me every step of the way. We drove to the hospital in silence and sat outside a packed waiting room waiting to be called.

When my name was eventually called, Mam came in with me to the room. An elderly man sat across from us with my file on his desk in front of him. My mother grabbed my hand and smiled at me. Again, I felt the calmness wash over me. "There's good news and bad news Ms. Hand," he said. "The good news is you don't have cancer." A rush of relief swept through me. My mother kept saying 'Thank God, Thank God!'

'The bad news is you do seem to have a fibro adenoma, A sizeable tumour growing in your breast. With the history of breast cancer in your family, it would be advisable to remove it but it is not of concern at the moment. It is your decision if you would like to have the surgery.' My mother was still registering the 'no cancer' news and didn't really hear what had been said afterwards so the doctor had to repeat himself. There was nothing to consider. I wanted the tumour out.

We were sent to a consultant who then made an appointment for the surgery. Two weeks later I returned to St Vincent's and had the lump removed. The surgery had its own complications but in the end, I was fine, absolutely fine.

I was off work again for a short recovery time and it was then that I decided to make my bucket list. I felt like I had been given a kick up the backside to really look at myself and my life. Was I doing what I wanted to be doing? Had I seen the places I wanted to see? Was I even really living??

My life changed forever after those few months. When you are not well, you promise yourself to never take your health for granted again and that you will do whatever it takes to get better and realise the important things in life. That was exactly what I did. I made an 'Escape Plan,' as I called it. I gave myself two more years of teaching, an opportunity to save enough to go travelling. I also wanted to look into my dream job in media and to spend more time with my loved ones.

During those two years, my father became ill with bowel cancer. It was a very difficult time for all of us and he had a tough few months of surgery and follow up treatments. I remember telling him that I had that same warm feeling of calmness when I was told about his illness and that it would be absolutely fine. I was starting to trust in my subtle sense a lot more and that, with both of our diagnosis, there had been no prior warning but that this calmness must mean something. After surgery and chemotherapy he was given the all clear in November

2012. We were all elated and celebrated with a big party for his birthday that same month. It brought us closer together. Both of us go for our regular six month check-ups now and are not afraid to talk about anything that may be worrying us. I would highly advise anyone who may be reading this and going through something similar to believe in that calmness that can wash over you. I believe it is an angel or loved one from the parallel world putting their arms around you to protect you. Trust your gut and say a wee prayer.

A Troubled Spirit

I spoke about energies and our connection to each other. Unfortunately it is not always a happy energy that comes into people's lives. I have only had one bad, truly scary experience with a spirit so far. It happened in my sister's rental accommodation while she was studying in Maynooth. She was sharing a house with two of her girlfriends and had been complaining for a number of weeks that there were strange things happening in her house. One of the other girls had been hearing whispers at night time from the foot of her bed. Doors had been opening and closing by themselves. They were finding a clear jelly like substance in puddles on the floor at different times. There were scratch like noises being heard from the sitting room wall. The wall was not attached to the neighbour's house next door. The whole thing had gotten to the point where they were all afraid to stay in their own rooms at night and huddled up together in the bigger of the bedrooms.

Sarah had asked me if I could do anything to help or knew of anybody but I didn't know anyone who could help. I suggested a priest should come out and bless the house but to keep her and the girls assured that they weren't going crazy, I said I would visit them and see things for myself.

I was in a relationship with an army officer at the time and he was also curious to see exactly what was going on so on a cold wet November evening we drove over to Sarah's house. As soon as I crossed the threshold, I could feel the heavy energy like a weight pushing down on me and I knew there was an unhappy spirit in the building. I asked Sarah to show me around the rooms and when we got to the smallest of the bedrooms, I could feel a coldness all around me. I asked if this was the room in which the voices were heard and she said yes. We sat on the bed for a few minutes and I got the feeling that this was an immature spirit. It was something to do with that room and the fact that this spirit didn't want anyone in it.

I'm no ghost hunting expert, nor do I see myself as someone educated in exorcism rituals but my natural instinct was to speak out loudly to whatever was causing the mischief. So, I called out. 'Who are you," I asked. Sarah nestled her head under my arm. Nothing happened. I called out again. A green flash of light flew across the curtains. Then nothing. We both looked at each other and gasped. We called out again, together this time, but there was still nothing. I asked Sarah to sit with me in the sitting room and explain to me, again, what had been happening. Meanwhile, the other housemates and my boyfriend stayed in the kitchen chatting. We had closed all the doors and our only light in the sitting room was the open fire. As Sarah was telling me the story, I could hear the scratching noise on the wall behind me. It was a very steady scratch from the top of the wall right down to the bottom. Thinking to myself, this could be mice, if anything. I let Sarah continue. Then, suddenly, there were loud knocks at the sitting room door. We both jumped. My heart was beginning to pound at this stage and I opened the door to the kitchen to ask the others if they had heard anything. They hadn't. I went back into the sitting room and Sarah was visibly upset. She said this was exactly what they had been experiencing.

I started to speak aloud once more : "please leave this house. These girls have done nothing wrong. You are not welcome here.' BANG! The ironing board that was standing against the wall went crashing to the floor and a dog like growl came from behind Sarah's chair. Oh man, I thought, what are we dealing with here? Sarah was quite frightened at this point and I was starting to worry that I was only making things worse. A change of tactic was needed. "Whoever you are, we are sorry if you have been caused upset in this house. Please know that these girls mean no harm and wish to be left alone. Please leave this house now." I began to say a prayer and with that came another bang at the door. This time we heard screams coming from the kitchen. We jumped up from our seats and ran towards the kitchen door. When we opened it all we could see were three very frightened faces. I asked my boyfriend what had happened and he struggled to make sense. They were all pointing at the back door, a double glass door leading to the back garden. Sarah and I went over to it and just as we reached the door handle, I felt the sticky substance under my shoe. There was the clear jelly like substance right at the foot of the door. The guys started to explain that they had heard a bang and then a huge bolt of whitish-yellow light came out from under the sitting room door and then flew across the room out the back door. That it had blown the lights and put them in darkness which caused them to scream. I had no reason to doubt any of it, particularly my boyfriend. This was a grown man who was in the army. He would have seen some nasty sights in his job but here he stood in a house, in Maynooth, scared out of his wits. I had no words for any of them. I was as shocked and dumbfounded as they were. My only thought was to say another prayer that whatever it was it wouldn't return. We stayed for an hour or so after that and had a cup of tea with the girls (tea is a cure-all for anything!)

During the drive home we were silent in our own contemplation. It was only the next day the realisation of what had happened sank in. I felt like I had dreamt the whole thing. I called Sarah and she said they had all slept soundly in their own beds that night and nothing else had happened. I went to work and began to tell my colleague what had happened. As I was talking to her, she pointed down at my bracelet and asked what had happened. I looked at her puzzled and then glanced at my bracelet.

What was once pure silver was now extremely dark black in colour. Not only my bracelet but my golden ring had gone black as well! I took them off and examined them from top to bottom. What had happened?!

I brought them home to my local jewellery store where they had been purchased years before. The jeweller had no explanation for it. He said I must have been in close contact with chemical liquids or something. I hadn't been. Then it hit me, they were fine when I wore them to Maynooth that night but were black the following day. I told my sister and she couldn't explain it but she did say the house felt safer now and that whatever it was must have left the house when we did. I still don't have any explanation.

My mother had a similar experience of sorts around the same time. Not a troubled spirit in our home but more to do with her work. As I mentioned before, she was a primary school teacher for many years and taught 6th class for the majority of those years. One particular afternoon, she was teaching religion to her class. They were discussing the 'The Big Bang Theory'- how Science and Religion differ on the creation of the world. As she was speaking to her students, she felt a sharp pain in her right ring finger where she wore a gold signet ring given to her by her parents. When she looked down, her finger was beginning to swell and the ring was beginning to change shape. Her natural reaction was to try and get the ring off. She had to explain to the class what was going on as she was becoming a little panicked. When she did get the ring off, she placed it on her desk and she, along with the entire class, watched as it melted and twisted itself into a deformed shape.

The school chaplain was called down to the school to see what the fuss was about. When Mam explained what happened and showed him the ring, he simply asked her what she had been teaching at the time. She told him they were on the topic of the Big Bang Theory. He shook his head and said 'You might have angered a few spirits buried underneath your classroom. There are bishops and priests buried here and they were making their presence known. What does a bishop wear on his finger?'

She took the ring to the jewellers (pretty sure this jeweller thinks we're all crackpots by now!) and he couldn't understand what had happened. He said there was no physical way that body heat could melt a gold ring. There had to be a more mysterious answer. She never got that ring fixed.

Granny

Part Three

My Granny was getting older at this stage and it was beginning to show in many ways. She became a little forgetful, more aches and pains and was starting to leave the house less and less. After the telephone incident, her family decided she needed to be cared for a little more so everybody took their turn spending a night with her in her home or taking her out for dinner. By now, I had left my teaching job, ended my relationship with the army officer, given up my rental apartment in Dublin and had moved home to Monaghan for a little while before going on my travels around the world. It was a fresh start. I stuck to my 'Escape Plan' and achieved some of the items on my bucket list in the space of a few months.

One such item on the list, as I mentioned before, was spending more time with my loved ones including my two Grandmothers –Granny & Seannaí. I always spent the night of the 23rd December with Granny and then she would come out to our house for all of the Christmastime. I loved that time of year with her. She used to make rasher sandwiches and we'd watch the golden oldies on TV like *Calamity Jane, The Sound of Music* or our favourite - *Mary*

Poppins. My sister and I used to sing 'Feed the Birds' continuously to her, which sometimes drove her up the walls as we would change the lyrics to suit ourselves!

On the night of the 23rd of December 2014, Granny had gone to sleep in her own room; I settled into the spare room and fell asleep quite quickly. I was awakened in the middle of the night to sounds coming from downstairs. I thought it was Granny but then I heard her snoring from her own room. Once again, I didn't know what to do, felt useless. I was frozen in the bed and couldn't move. What if we were being robbed?? Then, just as soon as the noise had come, it was gone again. Nothing but silence. I said a prayer and turned over in the bed thinking I was hearing things. A minute later, the blow heater in my room turned itself on. This was a switch heater that needed to be physically pushed on and off. I jumped in the bed and looked around the room. No one there. I could still hear her snoring next door. I turned off the heater and lay awake the rest of the night. There was definitely a spirit playing tricks on me and I reckon it was my Grandfather, who I had never met. He was coming in and out of both worlds letting us know he was about.

I didn't say anything to Gran the following day but when I brought it up with my sister, she said she had heard similar noises the nights she had stayed over, as had my brother! They described it as someone who was just walking in and out of the rooms like it was their own home. It had to be Granda!

In March 2015, I had a vivid dream that Granny was not going to be around for much longer. I was dressed in black standing with my extended family around a coffin in our local church. There was no sign of Granny or Mam's oldest sister Marian in the dream so I guessed it had to be one of them.

By this time my sister had moved to Chicago and was settling into her new life in the States. She was deeply missed by all of us and I know she was homesick more than a little, especially for her two grannies. We'd keep her up to date via skype and photos/videos regularly but, of course, it was never as good as the real thing. I rang her soon after my dream and told her that she needed to come home and say her goodbyes to Granny, that she may not get another chance to do so. She didn't question it. She trusted me wholeheartedly and booked her flight straight away. We kept it a surprise from my parents and when she arrived home in mid-April, it did us all the world of good. They had placed Granny in respite (care home) for two weeks as a break from looking after her so I drove Sarah out to see her. We both got a big shock when we saw how much she had changed in appearance and how her memory had deteriorated in the space of a few weeks. She had no idea who we were and it was confusing her to have us there so we left with our heads hung low. When we got into the car, we both cried. The woman we had grown up with, had never been without, was slowly leaving us. Sarah had her opportunity to say her goodbyes and went back to Chicago a few days later. There was a lot more crying at the airport.

On the 7th of May, I got a call from my Dad to come home from Dublin. Granny had taken a turn and was in Newry Hospital. The doctor had given her twenty-four hours and phone calls needed to be made. I sobbed my heart out the entire journey to Newry from Dublin that night. My best friend Ali called me on bluetooth and did her best to comfort me and keep me company the entire drive. When I landed at the hospital, I cleaned myself up and made my way to her room. She was in a private room away from the main wards. When I opened the door, I expected to see her on machines and in a coma. Nope! Not Granny! She was surrounded by all of my cousins, aunts, uncles and was sitting up in the bed with her arms crossed and the hair freshly permed. I thought 'wait a minute, did I hear wrong??' She knew who I was when I came in the door and gave me a huge hug. The old Granny was back! We chatted for a little while and slowly the room began to empty. The doctor said she was beginning to have organ failure and that it was only a matter of time, her being so old. We took it in turns to sleep next to her in the hospital, sing her favourite songs to her, read to her, pray and laugh with her for eight straight days. She wasn't going until she was good and ready!

On the seventh day of us taking turns to care for her, Mam and I were timetabled to take over from my aunt Meg. It was a Thursday afternoon and we sat either side of Granny chatting to Meg before she left. Suddenly, that faint feeling came, as if I were about to slip into a deep sleep. The entire room went a very bright yellow and I could feel a ferocious heat coming from the bottom of Granny's bed. There in my mind, I could see him. My Grandfather whom I have never met shuffling from side to side excitedly looking at my Gran. I began sobbing and my aunt raced across the room to me. My mother didn't move. She could feel it too and knew what was happening. She told Meg to wait and let whatever was going to happen, happen.

Granda looked so happy. He was like a little boy on Christmas morning. Behind him stood five silhouettes, dark shadows of different sizes all standing closely next to each other. Whoever stood in the middle was a very tall male form. And behind them, again, was the bright yellow light shining towards Granny. There, in the distance, came two more silhouettes walking together towards the group but they were helping each other to walk. One of them was poorly and the other was holding them up. It looked to be an elderly and another not so elderly woman together. The vision was gone after a few seconds and I was able to gather myself together. I looked over at my mother and tears were streaming down her face. My poor aunt wasn't sure what was going on but I explained what I had seen and said that whenever the two ladies finally reached the group of five silhouettes, Granny would go and that it would probably happen within twenty-four hours.

When I described the silhouettes, they thought it might have been Granny's brothers and sisters waiting for her. They couldn't figure out who the other two ladies were. Neither could I. I really didn't want to leave Granny that evening and I even begged Dad to take me back out to see her that night but we were all so tired that we fell asleep as soon as we got home. We slept through the night and were awakened by the phone ringing early the next morning. It was Mam's other sister saying it was Granny's time and we needed to come quickly.

I drove my mother and my brother over as fast as I could. While I was driving, the name Mary Ann came to me. I asked my mother about it and she said it was Granny's mother's name. I said the woman being carried by the other woman in the vision was a Mary Ann. Mam could only nod along. She was in a world of her own at that moment preparing to say her last goodbye to her mother.

When we got to Gran's room, nearly everyone was there and you could hear the raspy breaths coming from the bed. All of her children sat around her and held her. They spoke to her soothingly and said their goodbyes. We all cried and when my Dad came into the room, the air shifted. The bright yellow light came back from the corner of the room and I could see Granda stretch out his hand to lift Granny from the bed. All the silhouettes were together now, waiting for Granny to come and join them. She looked so different to the person lying in the bed. She was back in her fifties/sixties it seemed, with big chunky glasses on her. She took my grandfather's hand and looked back at what she was leaving behind. She had a worried look on her face and I said aloud to my mother – "You have to tell her it's ok, that you're all going to be ok and she needs to go." Typical Granny, always a Mammy first, looking out for her children. The whole room started willing her to go. And she did.

It was heart wrenchingly the most beautiful and precious thing I have ever seen in my life. Even now as I write, the tears are streaming down my face remembering the moment. She had a lovely death, surrounded by all of her family just as she had always prayed for.

Later that year when we were clearing Granny's house out, we found a picture of the Sacred Heart on a bedroom wall that had the names of all Granny's children. The first name on it was Mary Ann. I looked at Mam and asked who that Mary Ann was? She said it must be her sister, the aunt who was still sick as I mentioned before. Apparently she was called Mary Ann by birth but named Marian and that's what we'd all known her as, including my mother. It was Marian who was being carried by Granny's own mother in my vision. Both of them Mary Ann's!

This reaffirmed my belief that Marian is indeed in the twilight zone. It was very comforting to know that Granny was surrounded by *all* of her children when she passed over.

Gran made her new presence known in various ways over the months following her death. At her wake, my two cousins and I stayed up with her all night to keep her company. When one of my cousins began talking about an old argument that had happened between Granny and her sister years before, the crystal candlestick behind her coffin flew across the room straight at my cousin. I think it was Gran telling us to shut up because she never liked talking about it when she was alive, even though they had settled their differences years before.

Her birthday fell on the 17th June and my sister Sarah got in touch from Chicago. As she texted, I felt Gran next to me telling me I had to give Sarah a few messages. I wrote them all down and sent them to Sarah. It all made sense to her and gave her a lift, knowing she was being looked after from beyond.

In September of the same year, I woke up one morning in the apartment in Dublin with a strong urge to get in touch with my aunt Meg. I texted her after my breakfast and asked if she was about. Meg lived on the other side of Dublin city. We agreed to meet in town later that afternoon and I'm glad we did. We went to Eason's book shop, on O' Connell Street, and sat in the coffee shop chatting for ages. We talked about Granny a lot and how each of us had been since the funeral. I know it was tougher on Meg than some of the rest of us because she had spent so much of her life visiting Granny regularly, spending her Christmases' with us all, including Granny, in her hometown.

All that had come to an end when Granny passed away and Meg seemed a little lost. She spoke about how she was keeping busy doing various things like meeting friends, planning trips and going to the theatre. She was going to a show that very evening with a cousin of mine and then suggested that we should go to another show together before Christmas. I agreed and we looked up on the internet there and then what shows were coming to Dublin over the next few months. It turned out the next show was going to be *Mary Poppins* and the only date left available to us was the 23rd of December! Well I laughed out loud. Meg looked at me amusingly and asked what was so funny. I smiled and said 'Granny's brought us together today. She knew what that date meant to me and of all the shows to be on, that particular one with that particular song in it had to be on.' Meg laughed too and I think we both had a pleasant warm feeling of Gran's presence there and then. That feeling I got when I got out of bed that morning was Granny telling me to go out and meet Meg. She knew it wouldn't have happened otherwise. We went to the show on the 23rd and it was fantastic. When *'Feed the Birds'* was sung, I cried my eyes out. It felt very special. I haven't been able to listen to that song anymore. The nostalgia is a little too much to take, I guess.

In July 2016, Granny came to me again in a dream. She was resting her head on my lap as I sat in our sitting room with Sarah standing in front of the fireplace staring at us. Granny spoke and said 'You know what's coming.' I remember it being an immensely short dream and not thinking much of it when I woke up. I got a phone call later that day from Sarah to tell us she had just gotten engaged to her now husband Idas. I guess Granny was aiming what she said in the dream more at Sarah instead of me!

Granny pops in and out from both sides now and again, mostly when she is needed. But she is content in the Parallel World and doesn't need to do so as much anymore. We have to learn to let go as well. It's important that we grieve for ourselves but to also let the person go. They have become souls with a purpose elsewhere and respecting that can sometimes be hard for a person to accept, particularly in extreme circumstances but we have to trust that it's going to be ok. So, if you are holding onto someone who has passed on, remember they just want you to be happy and in achieving that, you are letting *them* go to the happiest place there is.

Sarah reminded me of something recently. Remember that number I asked Granny about all those years ago, number 97? Well, she was 97 years of age when she passed over. Coincidence?

The Unexplained

In June of 2015, a month after Granny had passed, I went to visit my aunt Marian in hospital. She is under twenty-four hour care in a beautiful ward with lots of friendly faces and lovely nurses. I was aware that this was the first time I would see Marian since her mother had passed and that I wasn't sure if she was aware of what had happened. She was awake when I stood by her bed and when I held her hand, I got a ferocious pain, like a thousand volts of electricity shooting through me, from my toes to my ribs. All I could do was look into Marian's eyes. She wouldn't let go of my hand and I was starting to feel faint with the pain. It was like I could actually feel her own discomfort in that bed. The pain of what she must have been and still is going through is heartwrenching. When she finally let go, I fell back against the wall and could feel my heart pounding out of my chest. I was so weak. I needed water and somehow managed to get myself out to the vending machine. I took a huge gulp of water and took out my phone. I rang my Dad in a state of panic and told him what had happened. He comforted me down the phone and told me to eat a chocolate bar or the like to get my sugar levels back up. He never doubted the incident for a moment and I was so grateful to speak to someone I trusted. Neither of us could explain it and even now I am not one hundred percent sure of what happened but I tend to think that Marian was trying to communicate her feelings in the only way she could.

Human contact is so important in any person's life. Every time I visit her now, I always put my hand on her chest above her heart and say a prayer and then on her head and cheeks, in a cupping sense, to let her feel a loving touch and the warmth of a loved one. She lights up every time and for a split second, it's like having the old Marian back. It's important that we show love to one another. A simple hug, holding someone's hand or even a smile across a room can change how someone might be feeling at that very moment. Don't be afraid to show your love.

Another unexplained experience happened in a family friend's home on two separate occasions. I will call this friend 'E'. The first time it happened was when my sister had come home from the states for a short visit, she wanted to surprise our friend so I drove her up to the house and there was plenty of screaming and hugging when 'E' opened the door to see Sarah standing there. We spent the entire evening in her sitting room chatting and laughing and as talk turned to more poignant stories, 'E' opened up about the death of her mother many years before. As she was talking, a black shadow walked in from the hall door behind her and vanished within seconds. I looked at Sarah and 'E' but they were continuing to chat and weren't aware of it at all, it seemed. I never said anything and put it down to a little tiredness I was probably feeling from all the running around that day. It was only as we were driving home after our visit that Sarah nervously asked me –'Do you know when 'E' was talking about her Mum earlier, did you feel anything come into the room?' My heart leapt. I looked over at Sarah and said yes. She went on to say 'I could have sworn I saw a black shadow come in from behind E's chair as she spoke.' It's crazy to say this but I was actually excited. Yes, excited, because finally, someone else had experienced something at the exact same time and way I had. I told her that was exactly what I had witnessed too and the pair of us wondered who or what it could have been. Sarah got in touch with E the following day and told her what had happened. E said she wasn't one bit surprised as she feels things in her home all the time and that over the years, her children had seen things too.

Not long after that, I was back in E's house again on my own this time to visit her daughter who I will call 'H'. We had decided to get a takeaway and have a long overdue catch up. We were sitting in the same room as last time and as were chatting, I felt the same presence come in from the hall. This time it was stronger and I could feel an almighty pressure pushing down on my head. I told H and as I was telling her, she said 'Aideen, your nose is bleeding.'

H left the room to get me tissues and when she returned I told her I needed to go home. I told her there was definitely something in that house and it might be a good idea to get it blessed. I had a headache after all the commotion and drove myself home and straight to bed. I told my father about it the next day and he reckoned it might be spirits from famine times or before as that house was built on the old famine road from the workhouse to the graveyard where bodies could have fallen from old trailers or wagons. It was a long shot I guess but I think he had a point. I still think there is more than one spirit attached to that land and definitely a mix of energies crossing paths in the house.

Dreams

Part Two

In December 2015, I was still living in Dublin but seemed to be moving closer to home as I was now on the Malahide Road. The apartment was right underneath the main flight path to Dublin Airport. The noise of the planes were a nuisance at first but, after a while, it became the norm. I was working as a freelance Media Presenter and Producer at this stage and found that if I was away on work related projects, I actually missed the sounds of the engines overhead whilst I slept. There was a strange comforting feeling to know that while I was tucked up in my bed, there were people flying to different countries right above me.

One night, around Christmas time that year, I had a very vivid dream about my Dad and a group of three people surrounding him as though they were protecting him from something. It was a woman and two men standing around him and I recognised one of the men as my late paternal grandfather. I had never met this man but my Dad had photos of him at home and I knew instantly that it was him. He looked a lot younger than in the photographs. I couldn't place who the other two individuals were. When I woke up, I remembered the dream so clearly and knew that because I had never dreamt of my grandfather before. This was obviously an important dream with a message of sorts.

I was a little reluctant to get in touch with my Dad to tell him but, after debating with myself, I gave in and sent him a text message asking was everything ok. I got an instant reply, which was unusual because it was quite late. He said he wasn't feeling ok and questioned why I had asked. As it turned out, he had seen something in his office at work that day that had unnerved him. Whilst sitting at his desk, he looked up to see a bright orb float from one end of the office to the other. He couldn't understand what it was as his office was quite small with little or no ventilation or windows so it couldn't be a reflection of sorts. He tried to make sense of the experience by saying he was probably tired and over worked but, deep down, I think he knew it was something else especially now that I was asking was everything ok. He asked me what I thought it could mean and I said it usually means that a loved one who has passed on is nearby. That's what I believed.

That then led me into telling him about my dream the previous night. By then it was no longer text messages back and forth, we were speaking in detail over the phone. I explained to him that they seemed to be protecting him from something. He had no idea what it could be but between that and the orb, we knew something unusual was afoot. When I described the people in my dream, I told him that the lady in it seemed to be quite well known or even familiar to my grandfather as was the gentleman, but more so the lady. Dad knew who they were straight away. He told me that when I got home that weekend, he would take me to his mother's house (Seannaí) and show me who they were.

I was intrigued to see what he was going to show me and when the weekend came round, I drove home quite giddily. I know it sounds crazy, but if you have doubted yourself for so long and then you have dreams that actually make sense to other people, you want to see it through and get an 'end result' so to speak. When I got home, there was no hanging about, we were straight up to my grandmother's house. Seannaí looked at us in bewilderment when we tried to explain what we were searching for and why but she helped all the same. She loves a good mystery like the best of us! Dad went to the press with all the old photo albums and took out boxes and boxes of old pictures. We went through at least a hundred photos before he found the one he was looking for. It was a large black and white official looking photograph. There were men in tuxedos and ladies in formal dress. They were arranged in three rows, some sitting and some standing. It looked to be taken in the 1930's or 40's period. Dad said "take a good look at that photo and tell me if you spot anyone familiar."

As I searched through the faces in front of me, I spotted my grandfather sitting in the front row. He looked exactly as I had seen him in my dream. Youthful and handsome as hell! I continued to look at the other faces and spotted another familiar face at the very back standing extremely tall and strong looking. I said aloud 'That's him, that's the other man in the dream.' Dad smiled at me and said 'Yes, but keep looking, is there anyone else there you recognise?'

There in the middle row of the photo was a woman who looked vaguely familiar but differently styled to the lady I saw in my dream. I pointed at her and said 'I think this is the woman in my dream but she wasn't exactly like this when I saw her. Are there any other photos of these people?'

Seannaí handed me a smaller photo this time of poorer quality and pointed to a woman standing away from a gathering of people in it. I laughed out loud. This was the woman I saw and this was exactly how I saw her. Short mouse coloured crimpy hair with eyes that had dark circles underneath. I asked was this the same dressy lady from the first photo and Dad replied that it was. It was the eyes that gave her away. She seemed pensive or distant in both.

When I asked who these people were, I was not expecting the reply I got. The tall gentleman was my grandfather's best friend. They had been friends for years and shared their hobby of acting in local pantomimes together. The photograph was taken after a show they had performed in together. When I asked about the lady, Seannaí spoke this time and said it was my grandfather's sister! She had been close to him also and it seemed natural that they would still be close in the next life.

I was gobsmacked. I had never seen or heard about these people before and yet here I was telling two people who had known them, that these individuals had come to me in my dream. We left Seannaí's house and drove home. On the way, I asked Dad what he thought it all meant. He didn't know. Neither did I at that point but one thing I did know, he was being protected by the ones he loved.

Shortly after that episode, Dad visited his GP for his regular check-up. When the test results came back, he was told that there were abnormalities with one of the results and he would need to go to hospital for further testing. We all knew what happened last time he was told such news so tensions were running high. There was worry in the air at home and one evening I sat with Dad and recalled the dream the few weeks before. I told him that I believed we had our answer to the reasoning behind the dream. He was being protected from whatever was coming and that I trusted wholeheartedly that his own father was going to make sure he was going to be ok. We had to believe in that or what other hope was there. It gave me that calmness again that everything was going to be alright. I trusted my subtle sense fully.

On the 1st Feb 2016 – Dad went into hospital for the tests. It was an uncomfortable experience for him but he was aware that it was for the greater good. Days passed afterward that seemed like months as we awaited news of what may or may not be. I never lost hope and kept reassuring Dad that he was protected. When the call finally came, we were given the good news that all was fine. The relief that surged through my body was probably nothing compared to what surged through his own. We were deliriously happy. I said a prayer and thanked those who helped from the other side many times. I visited my grandfather's grave afterwards and spoke to him at length too. I'm always thankful to those watching over us. You never know when you're going to need them and when you do, they will be there.

Another dream that came to me a few years back was after a good friend of mine had lost her other half to cancer. It was a very difficult time for her but she never gave up hope. Like Granny, she believed in prayer and her faith kept her strong. Her husband, - we will call him 'MJ' - was very young when he passed away and left a young family behind too.

I visited her and the family regularly after his passing and we confided in each other about a lot of things. She was aware of my subtle sense and was open to the idea of what it entailed, without doubting me for a second. It was a few months after the funeral when I had a strong dream about MJ and he took me on a little journey through my dream. There were three parts to it. If you have ever read or watched Charles Dickens 'A Christmas Carol' it reminded me a bit of the different spirits that came to visit Scrooge.

MJ showed me three different parts of his life that he called 'some of his happiest memories.' The first was set in large open fields with a farm nearby. He was a young boy running on the land, alongside a stream, with another young boy. They seemed like best buddies or even relations. They had sticks in their hands and smiles on their faces as they explored the fields around them. It was like I had an aerial view of their adventures.

The second part took me to a church yard. There stood MJ with a younger version of my friend next to him. It looked to be a beautiful day and they were dressed in summer attire. They seemed to be sharing a laugh together and looked so youthful and happy.

For the final part of the dream, MJ was sitting in front of me at a wooden table. He wore a white shirt with greyish trousers and had the biggest smile on his face, almost excited. He seemed to be around the age he had passed over at and looked fuller in body and spirit. He looked me dead in the eyes and said that he was very happy, that where he was, was like reliving all one's best memories over and over. He was able to watch over his family from there and was so proud of them. He looked blissful.

It was hard waking up from that dream. I knew I had to pass the message on and I was afraid it would cause upset.

It was still a raw time for his loved ones and they were trying to settle into a new normality. But I did what I believed was right and passed the message on to his wife.

I know it brought some comfort to her and the dream was so accurate that she found solace in knowing he was ok, and that the family was going to be ok. It was then that I knew how lucky I was to have this sense. To have the ability to help others if needed.

I am not a psychic nor am I healer or whatever title people might choose to go by. I am an ordinary person who sometimes gets a little extra help from the other side. I can't predict when these experiences will occur. I don't go looking to find spirits or attempt to predict the outcome of a particular issue. I don't believe I have seen angels like others have. That would be something completely different for me if I had or ever do in the future. I don't think I can really ever fully explain what it is that I have. What I do know is that my subtle sense has a mind of its own and it picks and chooses when to come to me. It knows when I am best ready to receive it and it knows how best to show itself to me. I have no control over it.

'And the Rest Will Come'

At the time of Granny's passing, I was working in TV and a good friend of mine, who I worked with, advised me to visit a kinesiologist friend of hers that had helped her through some tough times. I was reluctant at first but my friend insisted that there was so much going on in my life at that time, it would be good to speak to an outsider. I knew she was right and there was so much happening in every part of my life that I was feeling weighed down. So, I got in touch with the lady and she booked me in for an appointment the following week.

When the day arrived to meet the lady, I got in my car and drove over towards her home. The entire journey over, I had shooting pains up my arms as if I was having a heart attack. Then my thumb started to shake uncontrollably whilst my hand rested on the wheel. I pulled the car over and thought I had better call for help but the pains left just as soon as they had appeared and I put it all down to nerves. When I reached the house, I met her at the door and she took me into her therapy room where we sat and talked for ages. She gave me great advice and she, also, had the gift of seeing spirits. She told me Granny was next to me and that she was encouraging me to embrace my sense and write a book and that once I had written about it, 'the rest would come after' whatever that meant!

Before I left I decided to bring up the pains in my arm and why my thumb had gone crazy on the way over. I asked her was her father still alive? She said yes but that he wasn't well at the moment. I asked had he had shooting pains up his arm and she told me he had had a heart attack recently. I showed her my thumb and it was beginning to shake again. I asked was it to do with her father and she gasped aloud. He had been diagnosed with Parkinson's disease and it had started in his right thumb. She believed he was beginning his own journey. I never saw that lady again……until the day after I sat down to finally write this book.

In late 2016, my mother was diagnosed with an illness and I told her about my visit to this Kinesiologist and that it may do her some good to visit also. I drove her to Dublin myself and when I met the lady at the front door, it was like a rekindling of old spirits. We hugged and chatted for a short while and she asked had I written the book yet. I told her I had just sat down the day before to do it and would hopefully get it finished in good time. She repeated the same thing she had said to me two years previously - 'Write it and the rest will come.'

So here I am, finishing 'the book' and wondering what the future may hold for me. Why write it in the first place you may ask? Well, firstly, I always did as I was told by my Granny! But I also did it for myself. To let the young Aideen forgive herself for being scared and doubtful. I'm now happy in the knowledge that I am all the better for sharing my story with others. Also, possibly, it might give someone else a chance to let go of their doubts and know that there is more to us than this life. Hope is a wonderful thing and what do we have if we don't have hope?

Acknowledgments

There are so many individuals I would like to thank for all their help and support in writing this book. First and foremost my family. I am forever grateful to the Mammy and Daddy for allowing me to come home and write this book from where it all began. Your support throughout the process along with the cups of tea and home cooked dinners kept me motivated to finish the job! To my sister who has been with me every step of my journey so far, even when she moved across the pond. Go raibh maith agat Babygirl for never doubting me or allowing me to doubt myself. To my brother David, to Seannaí and my extended relatives, thank you for your love and understanding.

I wouldn't be here without the love of my friends who helped and pushed me to achieve my goals and reassure me that I was doing the right thing in sharing my life, especially Ali, Anita, Elaine & Cathal – you are legends. A special word of thanks to Lisa, my rock and the most positive, life – loving, happy individual.

And finally thank you for taking the time to read my story and hopefully it may be a little help to you on your own path of life. Remember – 'prayer is mighty'. If you are ever in doubt, trust your gut and believe in yourself. It's all part of this wonderful journey we call *Life*.

AH

Printed in Great Britain
by Amazon